Cambridge English:
Key for Schools
2

WITHOUT ANSWERS

Authentic examination papers from Cambridge ESOL

CAMBRIDGE
UNIVERSITY PRESS

University Printing House, Cambridge CB2 8BS, United Kingdom

Cambridge University Press is part of the University of Cambridge.

It furthers the University's mission by disseminating knowledge in the pursuit of education, learning and research at the highest international levels of excellence.

www.cambridge.org
Information on this title: www.cambridge.org/9781107603134

© Cambridge University Press 2012

It is normally necessary for written permission for copying to be obtained *in advance* from a publisher. The candidate answer sheets at the back of the book are designed to be copied and distributed in class. The normal requirements are waived here and it is not necessary to write to Cambridge University Press for permission for an individual teacher to make copies for use within his or her own classroom. Only those pages which carry the wording '© UCLES 2012 Photocopiable' may be copied.

First published 2012
7th printing 2015

Printed in Italy by Rotolito Lombarda S.p.A.

A catalogue record for this publication is available from the British Library

ISBN 978-1-107-60313-4 Student's Book without answers
ISBN 978-1-107-60314-1 Student's Book with answers
ISBN 978-1-107-60315-8 Audio CD
ISBN 978-1-107-60317-2 Self-study Pack

Cambridge University Press has no responsibility for the persistence or accuracy of URLs for external or third-party internet websites referred to in this publication, and does not guarantee that any content on such websites is, or will remain, accurate or appropriate. Information regarding prices, travel timetables, and other factual information given in this work is correct at the time of first printing but Cambridge University Press does not guarantee the accuracy of such information thereafter.

Contents

Acknowledgements

A guide to Cambridge English: Key for Schools   5

Test 1	Paper 1	16
	Paper 2	28
	Paper 3	35
Test 2	Paper 1	36
	Paper 2	48
	Paper 3	55
Test 3	Paper 1	56
	Paper 2	68
	Paper 3	75
Test 4	Paper 1	76
	Paper 2	88
	Paper 3	95

Visual materials for Paper 3   96

Sample answer sheets   104

Acknowledgements

The authors and publishers acknowledge the following sources of copyright material and are grateful for the permissions granted. While every effort has been made, it has not always been possible to identify the sources of all the material used, or to trace all copyright holders. If any omissions are brought to our notice, we will be happy to include the appropriate acknowledgements on reprinting.

p. 17: Shutterstock/Anton Gvozdikov; p. 20: Thinkstock/© Jupiterimages; p. 57: Thinkstock/© Jupiterimages; p. 22: Thinkstock; p. 60 (M): Thinkstock; p. 80 (T & M): Thinkstock; p. 37: Shutterstock/HYPERLINK "http://www.shutterstock.com/gallery-715570p1.html" © mareandmare; p. 40: Shutterstock/HYPERLINK "http://www.shutterstock.com/gallery-187633p1.html" © Monkey Business Images; p. 42: Getty Images/ Julian Finney; p. 60 (T): Thinkstock/Brand X Pictures; p. 60 (B): Corbis/© Larraine Worpole/Arcaid; p. 62: Glow Images/Superstock; p. 77: Shutterstock/HYPERLINK "http://www.shutterstock.com/gallery-578401p1.html" © SeanPavonePhoto; p. 80 (B): Thinkstock/James Woodson; p. 82: Shutterstock/HYPERLINK "http://www.shutterstock.com/gallery-1093p1.html" © Mark William Richardson

Picture research by Out of House Publishing Solutions Ltd.

Book design by Peter Ducker MSTD

The CD which accompanies this book was recorded at dsound, London.

A guide to Cambridge English: Key for Schools

Cambridge English: Key for Schools, also known as *Key English Test (KET) for Schools*, is a qualification that shows a pupil can deal with everyday written and spoken English at a basic level.

Cambridge English: Key for Schools follows exactly the same format as *Cambridge English: Key*, also known as *Key English Test (KET)*, and the level of the question papers is identical. The only difference is that the content and treatment of topics in *Cambridge English: Key for Schools* have been particularly targeted at the interests and experience of school pupils, enabling them to:

- learn skills to communicate in English
- gain an internationally recognised certificate
- build confidence in learning a valuable life skill.

Cambridge English: Key for Schools is a version of *Cambridge English: Key,* also known as *Key English Test (KET)*, developed with exam content and topics targeted at the interests of school-age learners. It is at Level A2 of the Common European Framework of Reference for Languages (CEFR).

Cambridge English: Key has been accredited by Ofqual, the statutory regulatory authority for external qualifications in England and its counterparts in Wales and Northern Ireland.

Examination	Council of Europe Framework Level	UK National Qualifications Framework Level
Cambridge English: Proficiency Certificate of Proficiency in English (CPE)	C2	3
Cambridge English: Advanced Certificate in Advanced English (CAE)	C1	2
Cambridge English: First for Schools First Certificate in English (FCE)	B2	1
Cambridge English: Preliminary for Schools Preliminary English Test (PET)	B1	Entry 3
Cambridge English: Key for Schools Key English Test (KET) for Schools	A2	Entry 2

Successful *Cambridge English: Key for Schools* candidates receive a certificate that is accepted by colleges, universities, employers and governments around the world as proof of a learner's language abilities. Taking this exam is also useful preparation for higher level exams, such as *Cambridge English: Preliminary for Schools* and *Cambridge English: First for Schools*.

A guide to Cambridge English: Key for Schools

Cambridge English exams are developed and produced by University of Cambridge ESOL Examinations (Cambridge ESOL). Over 3.3 million people take Cambridge English exams each year in 130 countries. Globally, over 12,000 universities, employers, government ministries and other organisations rely on Cambridge English exams as proof of language ability.

Topics

These are the topics used in the *Cambridge English: Key for Schools* exam:

Clothes	Language	Shopping
Daily life	People	Social interaction
Entertainment and media	Personal feelings, opinions and experiences	Sport
Food and drink	Personal identification	The natural world
Health, medicine and exercise	Places and buildings	Transport
Hobbies and leisure	Schools and study	Travel and holidays
House and home	Services	Weather

Overview of the exam

Paper	Name	Timing	Content	Test focus
Paper 1	Reading/Writing	1 hour 10 minutes	Nine parts: Five parts (Parts 1–5) test a range of reading skills with a variety of texts, ranging from very short notices to longer continuous texts. Parts 6–9 concentrate on testing basic writing skills.	Assessment of candidates' ability to understand the meaning of written English at word, phrase, sentence, paragraph and whole text level. Assessment of candidates' ability to produce simple written English, ranging from one-word answers to short pieces of continuous text.
Paper 2	Listening	30 minutes (including 8 minutes transfer time)	Five parts ranging from short exchanges to longer dialogues and monologues.	Assessment of candidates' ability to understand dialogues and monologues in both informal and neutral settings on a range of everyday topics.
Paper 3	Speaking	8–10 minutes per pair of candidates	Two parts: In Part 1, candidates interact with an examiner; in Part 2 they interact with another candidate.	Assessment of candidates' ability to answer and ask questions about themselves and about factual non-personal information.

Paper 1: Reading and Writing

Preparing for the Reading section

To prepare for the Reading section, you should read the type of English used in everyday life, for example, short magazine articles, advertisements, instructions, etc. It is also a good idea to practise reading short messages, including notes, emails and cards. Remember, you won't always need to understand every word to be able to do a task in the exam.

Before the exam, think about the time you need to do each part and check you know how to record your answers on the answer sheet (see page 104).

Marks

Each item carries one mark, except for question 56 (Part 9), which is marked out of 5. This paper represents 50% of the total marks for the whole examination.

Reading			
Part	Task type and format	Task focus	Number of questions
1	Matching. Matching five prompt sentences to eight notices, plus one example.	Gist understanding of real-world notices. Reading for main message.	5
2	Three-option multiple-choice sentences. Five sentences (plus an integrated example) with connecting link of topic or storyline.	Lexical. Reading and identifying appropriate vocabulary.	5
3	Three-option multiple-choice. Five discrete three-option multiple-choice items (plus an example) focusing on verbal exchange patterns. **AND** Matching. Five matching items (plus an integrated example) in a continuous dialogue, selecting from eight possible responses.	Functional language. Reading and identifying appropriate response.	10
4	Right/Wrong/Doesn't say **OR** three-option multiple-choice. One long text or three short texts adapted from authentic newspaper and magazine articles. Seven three-option multiple-choice items or seven Right/Wrong/Doesn't say items, plus an integrated example.	Reading for detailed understanding and main idea(s).	7
5	Multiple-choice cloze. A text adapted from an original source, for example, encyclopaedia entries, newspaper and magazine articles. Eight three-option multiple-choice items, plus an integrated example.	Reading and identifying appropriate structural word (auxiliary verbs, modal verbs, determiners, pronouns, prepositions, conjunctions, etc.).	8

Preparing for the Writing section

To prepare for the Writing section, you should take the opportunity to write short messages in real-life situations, for example, to your teacher or to other students. These can include invitations, apologies for missing a class, notices about lost property, etc. They can be handwritten or sent as an email.

Before the exam, think about the time you need to do each part and check you know how to record your answers on the answer sheet (see page 105).

Writing			
Part	Task type and format	Task focus	Number of questions
6	Word completion. Five dictionary definition type sentences (plus one integrated example). Five words to identify and spell.	Reading and identifying appropriate lexical item, and spelling.	5
7	Open cloze. Text of type candidates could be expected to write, for example, a short letter or email. Ten spaces to fill with one word (plus an integrated example) which must be spelled correctly.	Reading and identifying appropriate word with focus on structure and/or lexis.	10
8	Information transfer. Two short authentic texts (emails, adverts, etc.) to prompt completion of an output text (form, note, etc.). Five spaces to fill on output text with one or more words or numbers (plus an integrated example).	Reading and writing down appropriate words or numbers with focus on content and accuracy.	5
9	Guided writing. Either a short input text or rubric to prompt a written response. Three messages to communicate in writing.	Writing a short message, note, email or postcard of 25–35 words.	1

Part 6

This part is about vocabulary. You have to produce words and spell them correctly. The words will all be linked to the same topic, for example, food. You have to read a definition for each one and complete the word. The first letter is given to help you.

Part 7
This part is about grammar and vocabulary. You have to complete a short gapped text of the type you could be expected to write, for example, a note and a reply, or a short letter. You must spell all the missing words correctly.

Part 8
This part tests both reading and writing. You have to use the information in one or two short texts, for example, a note, email or advertisement, to complete a document such as a form, notice, diary entry, etc. You will need to understand the vocabulary used on forms, for example, surname, date of birth, etc. You will need to write only words or phrases in your answers, but you must spell these correctly.

Part 9
You have to write a short message (25–35 words). You are told who you are writing to and why, and you must include three content points. To gain top marks, all three points must be included in your answer, so it is important to read the question carefully and plan what you are going to write. Before the exam, practise writing answers of the correct length. You will lose marks for writing fewer than 25 words, and it is not a good idea to write answers that are too long.

Mark Scheme for Writing Part 9
There are five marks for Part 9. Minor grammatical and spelling mistakes are acceptable but to get five marks you must write a clear message and include all three content points.

Mark	Criteria	
5	All three parts of message clearly communicated. Only minor spelling errors or occasional grammatical errors.	
4	All three parts of message communicated. Some non-impeding errors in spelling and grammar or some awkwardness of expression.	
3	All three parts of message attempted. Expression requires interpretation by the reader and contains impeding errors in spelling and grammar.	Two parts of message are clearly communicated. Only minor spelling errors or occasional grammatical errors.
2	Only two parts of message communicated. Some errors in spelling and grammar. The errors in expression may require patience and interpretation by the reader and impede communication.	
1	Only one part of message communicated. Some attempt to address the task but response is very unclear.	
0	Question not attempted, or totally incomprehensible response.	

A guide to Cambridge English: Key for Schools

Paper 2: Listening

Paper format
This paper contains five parts.

Number of questions
25

Task types
Matching, multiple-choice, gap-fill.

Sources
All texts are based on authentic situations, and each part is heard twice.

Answering
Candidates indicate answers either by shading lozenges (Parts 1–3) or by writing answers (Parts 4 and 5) on an answer sheet.

Timing
About 30 minutes, including 8 minutes to transfer answers.

Marks
Each item carries one mark. This gives a total of 25 marks, which represents 25% of the total marks for the whole examination.

Preparing for the Listening test
The best preparation for the Listening test is to listen to authentic spoken English for your level. Apart from understanding spoken English in class, other sources include: films, TV, DVDs, songs, the internet, English clubs, and other speakers of English, such as tourists, guides, friends and family.

You will hear the instructions for each task on the recording and see them on the exam paper. There are pauses in the recording to give you time to look at the questions and to write your answers. You should write your answers on the question paper as you listen. You will have eight minutes at the end of the test to transfer your answers to the answer sheet (see page 106). Make sure you know how to do this and that you check your answers carefully.

Part	Task type and format	Task focus	Number of questions
1	Three-option multiple-choice. Short neutral or informal dialogues. Five discrete three-option multiple-choice items with visuals, plus one example.	Listening to identify key information (times, prices, days of week, numbers, etc.).	5
2	Matching. Longer informal dialogue. Five items (plus one integrated example) and eight options.	Listening to identify key information.	5
3	Three-option multiple-choice. Longer informal or neutral dialogue. Five three-option multiple-choice items (plus an integrated example).	Taking the 'role' of one of the speakers and listening to identify key information.	5
4	Gap-fill. Longer neutral or informal dialogue. Five gaps to fill with one or more words or numbers, plus an integrated example. Recognisable spelling is accepted, except with very high frequency words, for example, 'bus', 'red', or if spelling is dictated.	Listening and writing down information (including spelling of names, places, etc., as dictated on recording).	5
5	Gap-fill. Longer neutral or informal monologue. Five gaps to fill with one or more words or numbers, plus an integrated example. Recognisable spelling is accepted, except with very high frequency words, for example, 'bus', 'red', or if spelling is dictated.	Listening and writing down information (including spelling of names, places, etc., as dictated on recording).	5

A guide to Cambridge English: Key for Schools

Paper 3: Speaking

Paper format
The paper contains two parts. The standard format for Paper 3 is two candidates and two examiners. One examiner acts as an assessor and does not join in the conversation. The other is called an interlocutor and manages the interaction by asking questions and setting up the tasks.

Task types
Short exchanges with the examiner and an interactive task involving both candidates.

Timing
8–10 minutes per pair of candidates.

Marks
Candidates are assessed on their performance throughout the test. There are a total of 25 marks in Paper 3, representing 25% of the total score for the whole examination.

Preparing for the Speaking test
Take every opportunity to practise your English with as many people as possible. Asking and answering questions in simple role plays provides useful practice. These role plays should focus on everyday language and situations and involve questions about daily activities and familiar experiences. It is also a good idea to practise exchanging information in role plays about things such as costs and opening times of, for example, a local sports centre.

Part	Task type and format	Length of parts	Task focus
1	Each candidate interacts with the interlocutor. The interlocutor asks the candidates questions. The interlocutor follows an interlocutor frame to guide the conversation, ensure standardisation and control level of input.	5–6 minutes	Language normally associated with meeting people for the first time, giving information of a factual personal kind. Bio-data type questions to respond to.
2	Candidates interact with each other. The interlocutor sets up the activity using a standardised rubric. Candidates ask and answer questions using prompt material.	3–4 minutes	Factual information of a non-personal kind, related to daily life.

Assessment

Throughout the Speaking test examiners listen to what you say and give you marks for how well you speak English, so you must try to speak about the tasks and answer the examiner and your partner's questions. The two examiners mark different aspects of your speaking. One of the examiners (the assessor) will give marks on the following:

Grammar and Vocabulary
This refers to the range of language you use and also how accurately you use grammar and vocabulary.

Pronunciation
This refers to how easy it is to understand what you say. You should be able to say words and sentences that are easy to understand.

Interactive Communication
This refers to how well you can talk about a task, and to your partner and the examiner. It also refers to whether you can ask for repetition or clarification if needed.

A2 Band	Grammar and Vocabulary	Pronunciation	Interactive Communication
5	• Shows a good degree of control of simple grammatical forms. • Uses a range of appropriate vocabulary when talking about everyday situations.	• Is mostly intelligible, and has some control of phonological features at both utterance and word levels.	• Maintains simple exchanges. • Requires very little prompting and support.
4	*Performance shares features of Bands 3 and 5.*		
3	• Shows sufficient control of simple grammatical forms. • Uses appropriate vocabulary to talk about everyday situations.	• Is mostly intelligible, despite limited control of phonological features.	• Maintains simple exchanges, despite some difficulty. • Requires prompting and support.
2	*Performance shares features of Bands 1 and 3.*		
1	• Shows only limited control of a few grammatical forms. • Uses a vocabulary of isolated words and phrases.	• Has very limited control of phonological features and is often unintelligible.	• Has considerable difficulty maintaining simple exchanges. • Requires additional prompting and support.
0	*Performance below Band 1.*		

The examiner asking the questions (the interlocutor) gives marks for how well you do overall, using a Global Achievement scale.

A guide to Cambridge English: Key for Schools

A2 Band	Global Achievement
5	• Handles communication in everyday situations, despite hesitation. • Constructs longer utterances but is not able to use complex language except in well-rehearsed utterances.
4	*Performance shares features of Bands 3 and 5.*
3	• Conveys basic meaning in very familiar everyday situations. • Produces utterances which tend to be very short – words or phrases – with frequent hesitation and pauses.
2	*Performance shares features of Bands 1 and 3.*
1	• Has difficulty conveying basic meaning even in very familiar everyday situations. • Responses are limited to short phrases or isolated words with frequent hesitation and pauses.
0	*Performance below Band 1.*

Further information

The information in this practice book is designed to give an overview of *Cambridge English: Key for Schools*. For a full description of all of the Cambridge ESOL exams, including information about task types, testing focus and preparation, please see the relevant handbooks which can be obtained from Cambridge ESOL at the address below or from the website: www.CambridgeESOL.org

University of Cambridge ESOL Examinations
1 Hills Road
Cambridge CB1 2EU
United Kingdom
Telephone: +44 1223 553355
Fax: +44 1223 460278
Email: ESOLHelpdesk@CambridgeESOL.org

Test 1

PAPER 1 READING AND WRITING (1 hour 10 minutes)

PART 1
QUESTIONS 1–5

Which notice (**A–H**) says this (**1–5**)?
For questions **1–5**, mark the correct letter **A–H** on your answer sheet.

Example:

0   You can listen to this in different languages.   *Answer:*   [0] A ■ B ☐ C ☐ D ☐ E ☐ F ☐ G ☐ H ☐

---

1   You do not have to pay extra to go here.

A Guide to the museum on CD
French/English
£2.50

B CLASSROOM CHANGE
2 – 3 p.m. German Class
Now in room 102

2   This is the latest time you can go inside this place.

C Castle Garden
Free entrance with your castle ticket

3   You can bring your own food here.

D MUSEUM TOURS IN ENGLISH
EVERY HOUR
MEET AT INFORMATION DESK

4   A guide will take you around this building.

E You can only eat food bought in the museum café

F Groups/Schools:
Eat your picnic lunches at these tables

5   If you buy a ticket early, it will be cheaper.

G East Park
Next month's concert
Book now – pay only £20

H Museum closes at 5 p.m.
Last ticket sold at 4.30 p.m.

PART 2

QUESTIONS 6–10

Read the sentences about a picnic.

Choose the best word (**A**, **B** or **C**) for each space.

For questions **6–10**, mark **A**, **B** or **C** on your answer sheet.

Example:

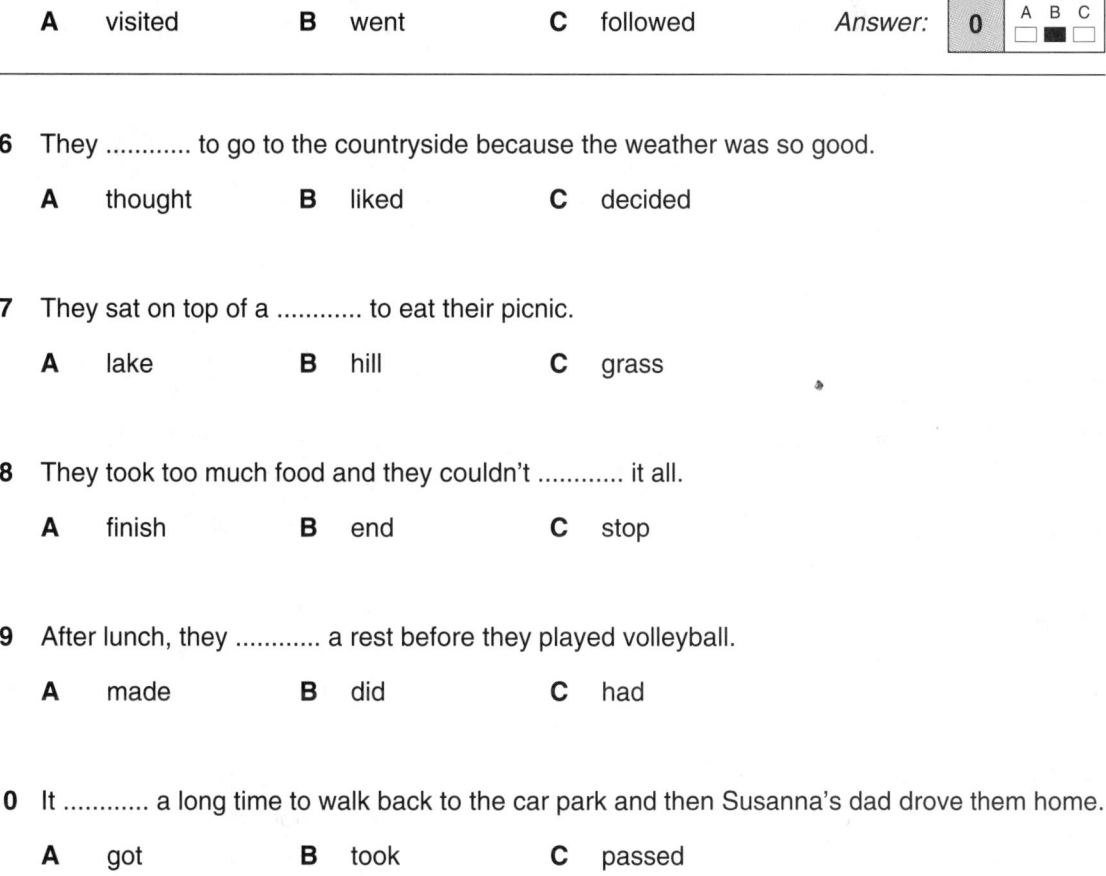

0 Last weekend, Susanna .... on a picnic with some friends.

   A visited   **B** went   **C** followed   *Answer:* 0 [A ■B C]

---

6 They .... to go to the countryside because the weather was so good.

   A thought   **B** liked   **C** decided

7 They sat on top of a .... to eat their picnic.

   A lake   **B** hill   **C** grass

8 They took too much food and they couldn't .... it all.

   A finish   **B** end   **C** stop

9 After lunch, they .... a rest before they played volleyball.

   A made   **B** did   **C** had

10 It .... a long time to walk back to the car park and then Susanna's dad drove them home.

   A got   **B** took   **C** passed

17

Test 1

PART 3

QUESTIONS 11–15

Complete the five conversations.
For questions **11–15**, mark **A**, **B** or **C** on your answer sheet.

Example:
0

A New York.
B School.
C Home.

Answer: 0 ■ A B C

---

11 Have a good holiday.

A Yes, a little.
B Thanks, I will.
C Yes, I have.

12 Do you like Jane's new coat?

A It's a beautiful colour.
B I can't wear it.
C She bought it.

13 I don't feel very well.

A Well done.
B What about you?
C I'm sorry to hear that.

14 Could you close the window?

A I am certain.
B If you want.
C I hope not.

15 I can't repair your bicycle.

A That's all right.
B I'm so sorry.
C I don't want to.

QUESTIONS 16–20

Complete the conversation between two friends.
What does Josh say to Marta?
For questions **16–20**, mark the correct letter **A–H** on your answer sheet.

Example:

Marta:	Hello, Josh. It's good to see you. How was your holiday?
Josh:	0 ....E......

Answer: 0 E

Marta:	Where did you go this year? To your uncle's again?
Josh:	16 ....
Marta:	No. Isn't it very cold there?
Josh:	17 ....
Marta:	Great! Did you take any photos?
Josh:	18 ....
Marta:	Yes, please! Did you stay in a hotel?
Josh:	19 ....
Marta:	That was lucky!
Josh:	20 ....
Marta:	I didn't know that. You must tell me more about it soon.

A Not really. In the summer you can even swim in the sea.

B We have some friends there and we slept at their house.

C No, but did you enjoy your holiday?

D Yes, it was! Hotels are very expensive there.

E It was great, thanks.

F Lots. I'll bring them to show you if you like.

G We didn't have enough money.

H We did something different – we went to Iceland. Have you been there?

PART 4

QUESTIONS 21–27

Read the article about a company that helps children with their writing.

Are sentences **21–27** 'Right' (**A**) or 'Wrong' (**B**)?

If there is not enough information to answer 'Right' (**A**) or 'Wrong' (**B**), choose 'Doesn't say' (**C**).

For questions **21–27**, mark **A**, **B** or **C** on your answer sheet.

Children's Voice

Children's Voice began in 2000 as a magazine written by children. It was the idea of a New York businessman called Sam Harris. He thought that people should listen to what children had to say. Harris soon found that adult newspapers were interested in the children's writing. He decided to close the magazine and started selling the children's news stories to adult newspapers.

Now Children's Voice has offices all over the UK. Since 2005, the people who work at Children's Voice have helped over 500 children with their writing. Many of these children have written news stories and programmes for TV and radio. The children, who must be aged 8–18, write about anything they think is important. Children's Voice shows them how to make their work good enough for publication.

Children's Voice is not really interested in finding school children who want to become journalists when they grow up. They want children to think for themselves and they want adults outside their schools to listen to them. They are really pleased that some of their writers are from poorer families and these children are often invited by national newspapers to write about the problems in their lives.

Paper 1 Reading and Writing

Example:

0   Children's Voice first started in 2000.

   A   Right   **B**   Wrong   **C**   Doesn't say   *Answer:*   0   A ■ B ☐ C ☐

---

21   Sam Harris believed it was important for people to know what children think.

   A   Right   **B**   Wrong   **C**   Doesn't say

22   Adult newspapers bought stories from Children's Voice.

   A   Right   **B**   Wrong   **C**   Doesn't say

23   The children are paid well for their work at Children's Voice.

   A   Right   **B**   Wrong   **C**   Doesn't say

24   Children's Voice tells the children what to write about.

   A   Right   **B**   Wrong   **C**   Doesn't say

25   Children's Voice would like their young writers to find jobs as journalists.

   A   Right   **B**   Wrong   **C**   Doesn't say

26   Children who write for Children's Voice get better in many school subjects.

   A   Right   **B**   Wrong   **C**   Doesn't say

27   Children's Voice is only for children from poorer families.

   A   Right   **B**   Wrong   **C**   Doesn't say

PART 5

QUESTIONS 28–35

Read the article about turtles.

Choose the best word (**A**, **B** or **C**) for each space.

For questions **28–35**, mark **A**, **B** or **C** on your answer sheet.

Turtles

Turtles spend most of their life (**0**) ………… the sea. They have a hard shell over their body and they can pull their head, arms and legs inside the shell (**28**) ………… they are in danger. Turtles (**29**) ………… live for one hundred years and grow up to two metres long. (**30**) ………… year, the mother turtle swims to a beach to lay her eggs. (**31**) ………… a month later, the eggs break open and the baby turtles (**32**) ………… to get into the sea. They are very small and (**33**) ………… have problems getting to the water.

Several years later, (**34**) ………… baby turtles will return to the same beach to lay their eggs. People think they find the way by following the light (**35**) ………… the moon or the stars.

Example:

| 0 | **A** | in | **B** | for | **C** | on | *Answer:* | 0 A■ B☐ C☐ |

28	**A**	but	**B**	if	**C**	so
29	**A**	soon	**B**	already	**C**	often
30	**A**	Each	**B**	Some	**C**	Other
31	**A**	Above	**B**	At	**C**	About
32	**A**	tried	**B**	try	**C**	trying
33	**A**	every	**B**	any	**C**	many
34	**A**	these	**B**	this	**C**	them
35	**A**	by	**B**	from	**C**	with

Test 1

PART 6

QUESTIONS 36–40

Read the descriptions of some places.
What is the word for each one?
The first letter is already there. There is one space for each other letter in the word.
For questions **36–40**, write the words on your answer sheet.

Example:

0   You can buy all the food you need for a week here.   s _ _ _ _ _ _ _ _ _ _

Answer: | 0 | supermarket |

36   You can watch a football match or a sports competition here.   s _ _ _ _ _ _

37   You go to this place to see actors in a play.   t _ _ _ _ _ _

38   People work in this place and may make cars or bicycles there.   f _ _ _ _ _ _

39   It can be hard to climb this, but you can see a lot from the top.   m _ _ _ _ _ _ _

40   This is a place in the countryside with lots of trees.   f _ _ _ _ _

PART 7

QUESTIONS 41–50

Complete the email.

Write ONE word for each space.

For questions **41–50**, write the words on your answer sheet.

Example: | **0** | to |

| **From:** | Gianni |
| **To:** | Kim |

Hi Kim,

I have some great news (**0**) .... tell you. Our town had a big rock concert (**41**) .... Sunday. I went (**42**) .... some friends from school and we listened to great music (**43**) .... day. There (**44**) .... six bands and over five thousand people came.

At the end (**45**) .... the concert, our school music teacher asked the guitar player from one of the bands to visit our school the (**46**) .... day. He agreed and we all had a wonderful time!

He stayed more (**47**) .... three hours and played a (**48**) .... of songs. He told (**49**) .... something interesting about his guitar, too – Bryan Adams gave (**50**) .... to him!

PART 8

QUESTIONS 51–55

Read the party invitation and the email.
Fill in the information in Flora's notes.
For questions **51–55**, write the information on your answer sheet.

Come to my
14th Birthday Party
on May 10 (4–9 p.m.)

At:
Silver Beach Club

Beach games and food

Bring some CDs!

Clara

From:	Sandra
To:	Flora

It's Clara's birthday on Thursday 8th May, but her party is on Saturday. Dad says it'll take 30 minutes to get there in the car so we'll leave at 3.30 p.m. Come to my house at 2.30 p.m. My dad has booked a taxi for us to get back.

I'm wearing my red shirt. Why don't you wear your new dress?

Flora's notes

Clara's party

Place:	Silver Beach Club
Date:	**51**
Time starts at:	**52** p.m.
What to take:	**53**
Wear:	**54**
Travel there by:	**55**

Paper 1 Reading and Writing

PART 9

QUESTION 56

Read the email from your English friend, Jo.

From:	Jo
To:	

Last night I had a really nice meal. What is your favourite meal? How often do you eat it? Who cooks it for you?

Write an email to Jo and answer the questions.
Write **25–35** words.
Write the email on your answer sheet.

27

PAPER 2 LISTENING (approximately 30 minutes including 8 minutes transfer time)

PART 1

QUESTIONS 1–5

You will hear five short conversations.

You will hear each conversation twice.

There is one question for each conversation.

For each question, choose the right answer (**A**, **B** or **C**).

Example:

Which is the girl's horse?

A

B

C

---

1 What will the weather be like tomorrow?

A

B

C

2 Which animals did Owen see at the zoo?

A

B

C

Paper 2   Listening

3   Which fruit does the girl buy?

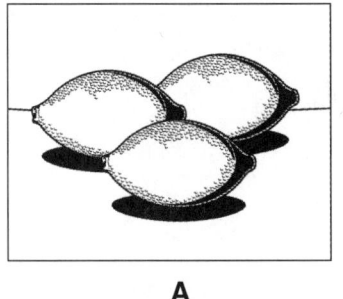
A

B

C

4   What time will the race start?

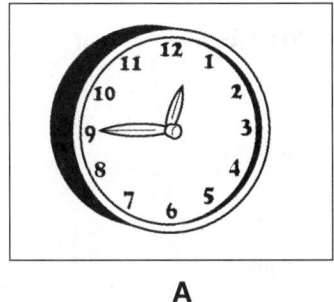
A

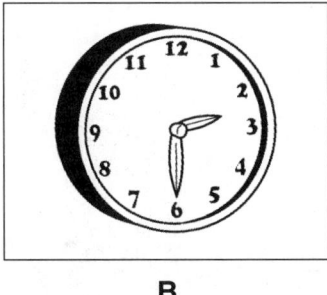
B

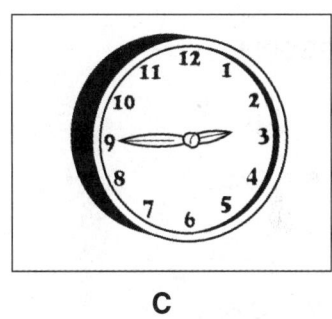
C

5   What is Tony's grandmother doing now?

A

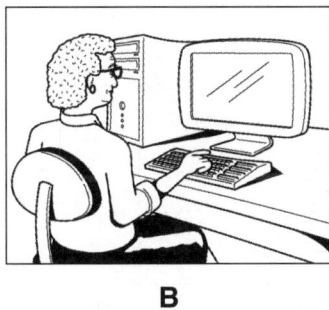
B

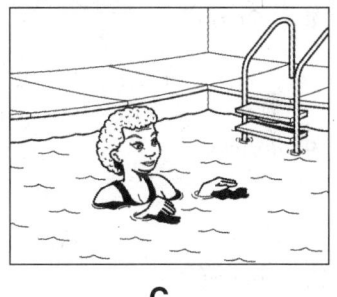
C

PART 2

QUESTIONS 6–10

Listen to Nick talking to a friend about the last day of his school trip.
What activity did each person do?
For questions **6–10**, write a letter **A–H** next to each person.
You will hear the conversation twice.

Example:

| 0 | Nick | C |

PEOPLE

6   Rob

7   Salina

8   Chloe

9   Vicky

10 Lizzie

ACTIVITIES

A   cinema

B   football

C   horse-riding

D   museum

E   reading

F   sailing

G   shopping

H   walking

PART 3

QUESTIONS 11–15

Listen to Kate talking to her friend, Joe, about piano lessons.

For each question, choose the right answer (**A**, **B** or **C**).

You will hear the conversation twice.

Example:

0 Kate has had piano lessons for

    A five years.

    (B) six years.

    C nine years.

---

11 How much do Kate's piano lessons cost?

    A £8.50

    B £10.00

    C £10.50

12 Kate's teacher tells her to practise for

    A 15 minutes every day.

    B 30 minutes every day.

    C 45 minutes every day.

13 Kate likes playing the piano because she

    A is learning to read music.

    B finds it easy.

    C can play music she enjoys.

14 Kate says her teacher is

    A   young.

    B   kind.

    C   famous.

15 Kate says she will

    A   give Joe piano lessons.

    B   let Joe practise on her piano.

    C   find Joe a piano teacher.

PART 4

QUESTIONS 16–20

You will hear a girl, Angela, telling a friend about a magazine competition.
Listen and complete each question.
You will hear the conversation twice.

Magazine competition

Name of magazine:	Teenworld
Competition prize:	(16) ....
You must be:	(17) .... years or under
Questions are on the subject of:	(18) ....
Send answers to:	(19) 30 .... Road
Date competition closes:	(20) .... March

Test 1

PART 5

QUESTIONS 21–25

You will hear a man talking on the radio about an adventure park.

Listen and complete each question.

You will hear the information twice.

Adventure World

Near:	Upton
Opens on:	(21) .... March
Price of a child's ticket:	(22) £ ....
Day of shows for older children:	(23) ....
New ride travels at:	(24) .... km per hour
New animal in the zoo:	(25) ....

You now have 8 minutes to write your answers on the answer sheet.

PAPER 3   SPEAKING (8–10 minutes)

The Speaking test lasts 8 to 10 minutes. You will take the test with another candidate. There are two examiners, but only one of them will talk to you. The examiner will ask you questions and ask you to talk to the other candidate.

Part 1 (5–6 minutes)

The examiner will ask you and your partner some questions. These questions will be about your daily life, past experience and future plans. For example, you may have to speak about your school, hobbies or home town.

Part 2 (3–4 minutes)

You and your partner will speak to each other. You will ask and answer questions. The examiner will give you a card with some information on it. The examiner will give your partner a card with some words on it. Your partner will use the words on the card to ask you questions about the information you have. Then you will change roles.

Test 2

PAPER 1   READING AND WRITING (1 hour 10 minutes)

PART 1

QUESTIONS 1–5

Which notice (**A–H**) says this (**1–5**)?
For questions **1–5**, mark the correct letter **A–H** on your answer sheet.

Example:

0   You can wear what you like on this trip.   *Answer:*   **0** A B ■ D E F G H

---

1   Bring this money before the end of the week.

2   If you arrive late, you will miss this trip.

3   You must take these things with you.

4   You need the right clothes for this trip.

5   Come to this if you want some information.

A   **School Trip**
Don't forget your lunch and a camera

B   **Trip to Fashion Museum**
£8.50
Please pay by 5 p.m. Friday

C   **Theatre trip for Class 3B**
Uniform not necessary

D   You may bring £5 to spend in the museum shop

E   **School skiing trip**
£450 – includes hotel, flights and skiing lessons

F   Meeting, 7.00 p.m. Tuesday
Find out about the camping trip

G   Everyone must wear warm trousers and boots for tomorrow's trip

H   **School Trip**
Bus leaves 8.15 a.m.
We won't wait for anyone!

PART 2

QUESTIONS 6–10

Read the sentences about a day at the zoo.
Choose the best word (**A**, **B** or **C**) for each space.
For questions **6–10**, mark **A**, **B** or **C** on your answer sheet.

Example:

0   Polly .... her mum, 'Can we go to the zoo?'

   A asked   **B** said   **C** spoke

Answer: 0 A ■

---

6   Polly looked at the zoo website to .... what time it opened.

   A understand   **B** decide   **C** check

7   The zoo has 300 different .... of animals.

   A things   **B** names   **C** kinds

8   The bus .... to the zoo was 40 minutes long.

   A journey   **B** return   **C** way

9   Polly .... lots of photographs of the animals with her new camera.

   A made   **B** took   **C** saw

10   Polly spoke .... because some animals don't like too much noise.

   A quietly   **B** carefully   **C** slowly

Test 2

PART 3

QUESTIONS 11–15

Complete the five conversations.
For questions **11–15**, mark **A**, **B** or **C** on your answer sheet.

Example:

0   Where do you come from?
  A New York.
  B School.
  C Home.

Answer: 0 **A**

---

11 I'm going swimming at the pool.
  A Are you swimming?
  B Can I come too?
  C When did you leave?

12 Isn't Holly in your geography class?
  A No, I'm not.
  B It could be.
  C I'm not sure.

13 It's time to turn off your computer now.
  A Just a moment.
  B Just now.
  C Just in time.

14 Do you want some orange juice?
  A I'd like water, please.
  B May I have a drink?
  C Yes, you are right.

15 That boy looks like my brother!
  A Did he know?
  B Do you think so?
  C Have you decided yet?

QUESTIONS 16–20

Complete the conversation between two friends.
What does Suzy say to Kristina?
For questions **16–20**, mark the correct letter **A–H** on your answer sheet.

Example:

Kristina: Hi, Suzy. Are you going to Miss Syms' basketball practice today?

Suzy: 0 .....C......   Answer: 0 [A☐ B☐ C■ D☐ E☐ F☐ G☐ H☐]

Kristina: I can't. Could you tell Miss Syms I won't be there today?

Suzy: 16 ....

Kristina: I've got to meet my mum in town.

Suzy: 17 ....

Kristina: Not today. I've got toothache and Mum's coming with me to the dentist.

Suzy: 18 ....

Kristina: Thanks. But say I can come to practice tomorrow.

Suzy: 19 ....

Kristina: And if we do well, we'll win the cup!

Suzy: 20 ....

Kristina: Miss Syms will be so happy.

A Good. We need to improve for our match against Hill School!

B What a pity! How did you do it?

C Yes, I am. What about you?

D Oh dear. I'll explain to Miss Syms why you had to go into town.

E Yes, she needs help with those.

F OK, but why can't you come?

G Yes, the first time ever for our team.

H Right. Is she taking you shopping?

PART 4

QUESTIONS 21–27

Read the article about very clever children.

Are sentences **21–27** 'Right' (**A**) or 'Wrong' (**B**)?

If there is not enough information to answer 'Right' (**A**) or 'Wrong' (**B**), choose 'Doesn't say' (**C**).

For questions **21–27**, mark **A**, **B** or **C** on your answer sheet.

Clever children

There are some special children, who are called child prodigies. They are unusually clever. They can, for example, write music or play chess at a very young age. No-one knows why they are so clever. There is nothing unusual about their parents or their families.

Sometimes, a child prodigy is good at more than one or two things. Francesca Contini looks like any other young teenager, but at 13, she's already started doing medicine at university. Francesca and her two older brothers are also excellent musicians and they have all played at concert halls in New York where they live. Their parents work in a supermarket. They have never been interested in music and they are very surprised by their children.

Twelve-year-old Peter Lee is already an excellent piano player. He is very bored at school, so in the evenings he teaches himself mathematics and science from books for university students. When he was five, he got first prize in a piano competition for children up to 18. At 10, Peter made his first CD. On it, he played many different kinds of music.

Example:

0   Some child prodigies can play chess when they are very young.

    A   Right   **B**   Wrong   **C**   Doesn't say   *Answer:* 0 A ■ B ☐ C ☐

---

21   People understand why some children are child prodigies.

    A   Right   **B**   Wrong   **C**   Doesn't say

22   The parents of child prodigies are very clever too.

    A   Right   **B**   Wrong   **C**   Doesn't say

23   Francesca looks the same as other girls of her age.

    A   Right   **B**   Wrong   **C**   Doesn't say

24   Francesca practises very hard when she has a concert.

    A   Right   **B**   Wrong   **C**   Doesn't say

25   Peter already goes to university.

    A   Right   **B**   Wrong   **C**   Doesn't say

26   Peter won a music competition at the age of five.

    A   Right   **B**   Wrong   **C**   Doesn't say

27   Peter's CD has been very popular.

    A   Right   **B**   Wrong   **C**   Doesn't say

PART 5

QUESTIONS 28–35

Read the article about a young tennis player.
Choose the best word (**A**, **B** or **C**) for each space.
For questions **28–35**, mark **A**, **B** or **C** on your answer sheet.

Laura Robson

In 2008, Laura Robson became (**0**) .... top 14-year-old tennis player in the world. She (**28**) .... the Wimbledon Girls' tennis competition that year, and was the (**29**) .... player there.

Born in Melbourne, Australia, Laura and her family moved to Singapore (**30**) .... she was only 18 months old. Four years later, the Robson family came to Britain and decided to live in Wimbledon, just five minutes away (**31**) .... the famous tennis club. It is no surprise that Laura started to play tennis immediately, at the age of six.

(**32**) .... people in British tennis believe that Laura will get (**33**) .... better. At the moment, she is spending a lot of time in (**34**) .... countries, practising with top tennis stars. 'I (**35**) .... to work hard,' she says, 'but I love every minute.'

Example:

| 0 | **A** | the | **B** | one | **C** | a | *Answer:* | 0 | A ■ B □ C □ |

| 28 | **A** | wins | **B** | won | **C** | win |

| 29 | **A** | young | **B** | younger | **C** | youngest |

| 30 | **A** | when | **B** | which | **C** | who |

| 31 | **A** | with | **B** | of | **C** | from |

| 32 | **A** | Much | **B** | Many | **C** | Any |

| 33 | **A** | quite | **B** | so | **C** | even |

| 34 | **A** | other | **B** | another | **C** | others |

| 35 | **A** | must | **B** | have | **C** | should |

PART 6

QUESTIONS 36–40

Read the descriptions of some words about the circus.
What is the word for each one?
The first letter is already there. There is one space for each other letter in the word.
For questions **36–40**, write the words on your answer sheet.

Example:

0   You may visit the circus with these people.   f _ _ _ _ _ _

                                                                        Answer: | 0 | friends |

36   You buy this before you go into the circus.   t _ _ _ _ _

37   These people move around to music and often wear beautiful clothes.   d _ _ _ _ _ _

38   At some circuses, you can see people riding these.   h _ _ _ _ _

39   This person wears lots of make up and will make you laugh.   c _ _ _ _

40   When it is dark, these make it possible for you to see the show clearly.   l _ _ _ _ _

PART 7

QUESTIONS 41–50

Complete the emails.
Write ONE word for each space.
For questions **41–50**, write the words on your answer sheet.

Example: | **0** | to |

| **From:** | Boris |
| **To:** | Lucia |

A new computer club is going (**0**) .... start next week. (**41**) .... is on Wednesdays at 5.30 p.m. The teacher (**42**) .... called Mrs Harris. Do you know (**43**) .... ? I think she's great. This week we are learning (**44**) .... the internet. Would you like to join the club?

| **From:** | Lucia |
| **To:** | Boris |

Thanks for your email. I like Mrs Harris very (**45**) .... but I have a music lesson from 5 o'clock (**46**) .... 6 o'clock on Wednesdays. If it's possible to change (**47**) .... time of my lesson, I (**48**) .... come! How much does the club (**49**) .... and how many people (**50**) .... there in the club?

PART 8

QUESTIONS 51–55

Read the advertisement and the email.
Fill in the information in Angela's notes.
For questions **51–55**, write the information on your answer sheet.

Bookworld
2 High Street

LANGUAGE CDs

French or German

Level 1 (beginners)
Level 2

CDs - £6
CD + book - £10

From:	Martha
To:	Angela

Can you get Leah a language CD for her 13th birthday? Her birthday is on 6th April but we don't need the CD until her party on the 10th. Her French is good but she doesn't know any German – she really wants to learn. I have tried City Books in Market Square but they don't have this CD, so you should try Bookworld instead.

Angela's notes

CD for Leah

Name of shop:	Bookworld
Language:	**51**
Level:	**52**
Cost:	**53** £
Date needed:	**54**
Address of shop:	**55**

Paper 1 Reading and Writing

PART 9

QUESTION 56

Read the email from your English friend, Jan.

From:	Jan
To:	

Let's go to the skate park tomorrow. Where shall we meet? What time shall we meet? How much money do I need for the skate park?

Write an email to Jan and answer the questions.

Write **25–35** words.

Write the email on your answer sheet.

47

PAPER 2 LISTENING (approximately 30 minutes including 8 minutes transfer time)

PART 1

QUESTIONS 1–5

You will hear five short conversations.

You will hear each conversation twice.

There is one question for each conversation.

For each question, choose the right answer (**A**, **B** or **C**).

Example:

Which is the girl's horse?

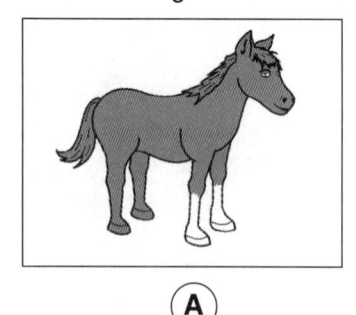

A   B   C

---

1 What lesson is the boy going to have this evening?

A   B   C

2 Where is the girl's mobile phone?

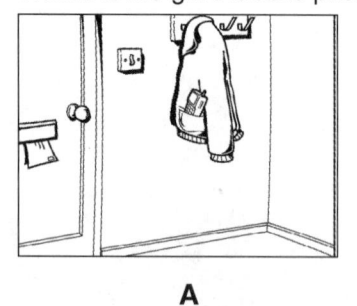

A   B   C

48

3 What time will the volleyball match finish?

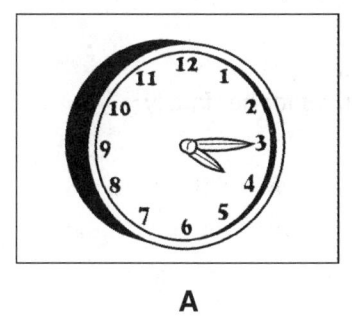

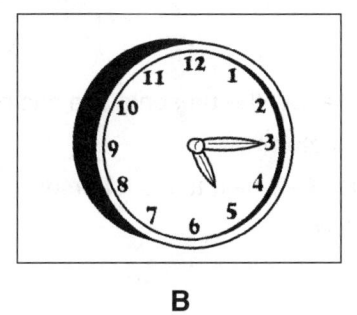

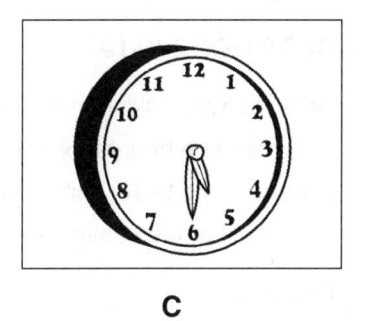

A   B   C

4 Which photograph did the girl take?

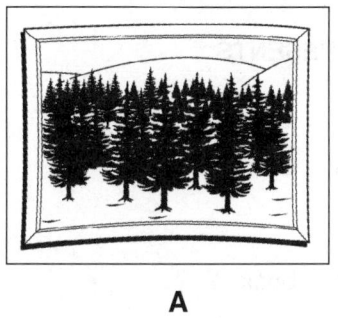

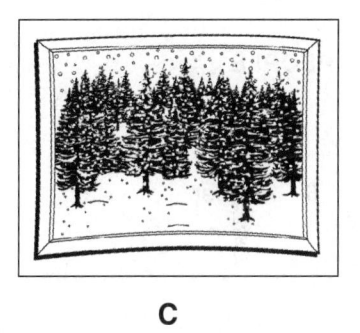

A   B   C

5 What is the boy eating with?

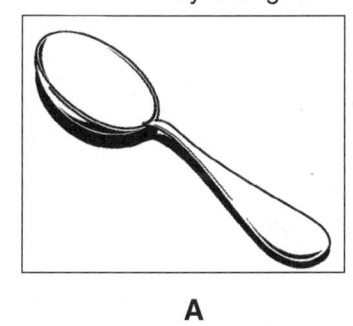

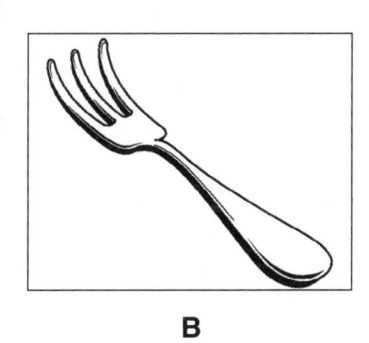

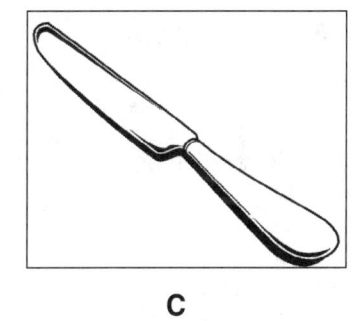

A   B   C

PART 2

QUESTIONS 6–10

Listen to Kate talking to a friend about the presents she has bought for her family.
What has she bought for each person?
For questions **6–10**, write a letter **A–H** next to each person.
You will hear the conversation twice.

Example:

| 0 | Mother | B |

PEOPLE

6   Father

7   Sister

8   Grandmother

9   Grandfather

10 Brother

PRESENTS

A   belt

B   book

C   glass animal

D   hat

E   picture

F   sunglasses

G   sweets

H   T-shirt

PART 3

QUESTIONS 11–15

Listen to Ben talking to Laura about playing in her band.
For each question, choose the right answer (**A**, **B** or **C**).
You will hear the conversation twice.

Example:

0   What music does Laura's band play?

    A   reggae

  (**B**) rock

    C   hip hop

---

11   The band needs someone to play

    A   drums.

    B   guitar.

    C   keyboard.

12   When is the band going to practise this week?

    A   on Monday evening

    B   on Wednesday evening

    C   on Thursday evening

13   At the moment, the band practises

    A   in a room at school.

    B   in a garage.

    C   at Laura's apartment.

14 Laura says the band will have its first concert in

    A August.

    B September.

    C October.

15 If there's a problem, Ben should

    A call Laura.

    B text Laura.

    C email Laura.

Paper 2   Listening

PART 4

QUESTIONS 16–20

You will hear a boy asking a girl about the school café.
Listen and complete each question.
You will hear the conversation twice.

School café

Café is near the:	Library
Opens at:	(16) .... a.m.
Best food is:	(17) ....
Price of most expensive meal:	(18) £ ....
This week, free:	(19) ....
Nicest member of staff:	(20) Mrs ....

Test 2

PART 5
QUESTIONS 21–25

You will hear a message about the films showing at a cinema.
Listen and complete each question.
You will hear the information twice.

Today's films

Morning

Name of film:	Gone with the Wind
Winner of 'best film' in the year:	(21) ....
Children must be:	(22) .... or older

Afternoon

Name of film:	(23) Happy ....
Price of child's ticket:	(24) £ ....
Cinema café closes today at:	(25) .... p.m.

You now have 8 minutes to write your answers on the answer sheet

PAPER 3 SPEAKING (8–10 minutes)

The Speaking test lasts 8 to 10 minutes. You will take the test with another candidate. There are two examiners, but only one of them will talk to you. The examiner will ask you questions and ask you to talk to the other candidate.

Part 1 (5–6 minutes)

The examiner will ask you and your partner some questions. These questions will be about your daily life, past experience and future plans. For example, you may have to speak about your school, hobbies or home town.

Part 2 (3–4 minutes)

You and your partner will speak to each other. You will ask and answer questions. The examiner will give you a card with some information on it. The examiner will give your partner a card with some words on it. Your partner will use the words on the card to ask you questions about the information you have. Then you will change roles.

Test 3

PAPER 1 READING AND WRITING (1 hour 10 minutes)

PART 1

QUESTIONS 1–5

Which notice (**A–H**) says this (**1–5**)?
For questions **1–5**, mark the correct letter **A–H** on your answer sheet.

Example:

0 Everyone in the football team should go here this afternoon.

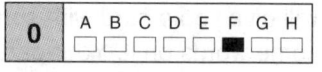

Answer: **F**

1 You can buy the sports clothes you need here.

2 The bad weather has stopped people playing sport.

3 If you want to do this sport, you should call this number.

4 It's not expensive to watch sport here tonight.

5 If you are a beginner at this sport, you can join these classes.

A See this evening's match at **Sunhill Stadium** for just $10

B Because of the heavy snow there is no baseball practice

C **City Pool** Do not leave anything in the changing room

D **Sale on today** *Half-price football shirts from $15*

E Stop watching and start playing! Join the tennis club ☎ 2857341

F **TODAY** Meeting for football team members in school hall – 4 p.m.

G **Love football?** Tickets for next week's match $30 Call 753981

H **Learn to swim** Lessons Tuesday and Thursday 7 p.m.

PART 2

QUESTIONS 6–10

Read the sentences about a summer camp for teenagers.
Choose the best word (**A**, **B** or **C**) for each space.
For questions **6–10**, mark **A**, **B** or **C** on your answer sheet.

Example:

0   Jay .... to Camp Belford during his summer holiday last year.

    A went   **B** spent   **C** left   *Answer:* 0 ■□□

---

6   There were lots of different activities for Jay to .... there.

    A make   **B** do   **C** play

7   The .... worked hard to make sure all the teenagers enjoyed themselves.

    A staff   **B** guests   **C** customers

8   Jay met lots of .... people from around the world.

    A right   **B** favourite   **C** interesting

9   On the last night, there was a big party and everyone .... fun.

    A had   **B** was   **C** got

10 Jay .... his friends all about the summer camp when he started back at school.

    A said   **B** told   **C** spoke

PART 3

QUESTIONS 11–15

Complete the five conversations.

For questions **11–15**, mark **A**, **B** or **C** on your answer sheet.

Example:

0

Where do you come from?

A New York.
B School.
C Home.

Answer: 0 [A■] [B☐] [C☐]

---

11 How about doing the homework together this evening?

A Me too.
B Great idea.
C I hope so.

12 Let me see that book!

A See you soon.
B What about you?
C Here you are.

13 Can I have some more of your cake?

A Yes, just a small piece.
B No, we couldn't eat there.
C Yes, I'd love to cook that.

14 I can't come to the party, sorry.

A Don't worry, I will.
B Of course you do.
C Oh well, maybe next time.

15 What kind of juice would you like?

A Can I have a drink?
B Do you want them, too?
C Have you got mango?

QUESTIONS 16–20

Complete the conversation between two friends.
What does Gina say to Tom?
For questions **16–20**, mark the correct letter **A–H** on your answer sheet.

Example:

Tom: Hi, Gina. I've got some tickets for a concert at the theatre this Saturday. Would you like to come?

Gina: 0 ....C....

Answer: 0 — C

Tom: A band called Starlings. They're very popular in America.

Gina: 16 ....

Tom: It's a kind of hip-hop. So what do you think?

Gina: 17 ....

Tom: Great. I'm sure you'll like them. It starts at 7.15.

Gina: 18 ....

Tom: Well, Dad's taking me so we can come and get you if you prefer.

Gina: 19 ....

Tom: What about meeting at the theatre café?

Gina: 20 ....

Tom: Excellent!

A So shall we meet at the theatre at 7.00?

B I usually prefer slow songs.

C Who's playing?

D OK, they do great pizza there.

E What time is that?

F I've heard of them but I don't know their music. What's it like?

G It's OK. I'm going shopping in town on Saturday so let's meet there.

H That sounds good. I'd love to come.

Test 3

PART 4

QUESTIONS 21–27

Read the article about teenagers who live in unusual homes and then answer the questions. For questions **21–27**, mark **A**, **B** or **C** on your answer sheet.

What a great home!
Three 13-year-olds describe their unusual homes

Paul

Living in a lighthouse is brilliant! The only problem is that it's a long way from school and my friends' homes, but they often come and stay. We have great football matches on the beach ten metres away. I'm having a party here next week and it'll be amazing. We moved here three years ago because Dad was tired of city life. He saw a TV programme about living by the sea and decided to do the same.

Nick

I can't imagine life in a normal house because I've always lived on a houseboat! We move it around and now we're on a river five minutes' walk from Dad's office and my school. My friends often come here and they all want to live on a houseboat now. You can watch TV and play computer games just like in a normal house, but it's more fun.

Harry

Dad's a builder and his company was making some underground houses. He decided to try one for a month but we've been here ten years already. It's an unusual house – it was even on a TV programme once. It can be cold but it's not dark because one side's open to the light. It's quiet here because of the earth around us. I invited twenty friends from school for my birthday. The music was loud but no-one could hear us. It was great!

Paper 1 Reading and Writing

Example:

0   Who does not talk about any problems about living in his home?

A   Paul
B   Nick
C   Harry

Answer: 0 A B C ☐ ■ ☐

---

21   Who has friends who say they would love to live in his house?

A   Paul
B   Nick
C   Harry

22   Who has had a very good party at his home?

A   Paul
B   Nick
C   Harry

23   Who has a very easy journey to school?

A   Paul
B   Nick
C   Harry

24   Who moved to his home because of his father's work?

A   Paul
B   Nick
C   Harry

25   Who says there is a good place to play games near his home?

A   Paul
B   Nick
C   Harry

26   Who has lived in his home for the shortest time?

A   Paul
B   Nick
C   Harry

27   Who lives in a home that was shown on TV?

A   Paul
B   Nick
C   Harry

PART 5

QUESTIONS 28–35

Read the article about teenagers in the 1950s.
Choose the best word (**A**, **B** or **C**) for each space.
For questions **28–35**, mark **A**, **B** or **C** on your answer sheet.

Teenagers in the 1950s

The 1940s in the UK were difficult years and most people had (**0**) .... little money. But in the 1950s many things changed. There were more teenagers and there were (**28**) .... jobs for everyone. Because most young people (**29**) .... lived with their parents, teenagers in the 1950s had more money than (**30**) .... before.

Between 1956 and '61 there were eight Hollywood movies (**31**) .... the word 'teenager' in the title. Actors (**32**) .... Marlon Brando and James Dean were the young stars of (**33**) .... time. On screen, (**34**) .... wore the same clothes as motorbike riders – leather jackets, T-shirts and denim jeans. This fashion soon (**35**) .... popular with teenagers around the world. Today, of course, these clothes are worn by everyone, not only young people.

Example:

| 0 | **A** quite | **B** almost | **C** very | *Answer:* | 0 | A B C |

| 28 | **A** enough | **B** such | **C** all |

| 29 | **A** yet | **B** too | **C** still |

| 30 | **A** already | **B** ever | **C** just |

| 31 | **A** with | **B** for | **C** by |

| 32 | **A** as | **B** from | **C** like |

| 33 | **A** a | **B** one | **C** the |

| 34 | **A** there | **B** they | **C** them |

| 35 | **A** become | **B** became | **C** becoming |

PART 6

QUESTIONS 36–40

Read the descriptions of some things you can hear or listen to.
What is the word for each one?
The first letter is already there. There is one space for each other letter in the word.
For questions **36–40**, write the words on your answer sheet.

Example:

0   You listen to this when you want to dance.   m _ _ _ _

Answer: | 0 | music |

36   To play this instrument, you hit it.   d _ _ _

37   When your friend calls you on this, you can   t _ _ _ _ _ _ _ _
     have a conversation.

38   This lives in a tree and sings beautifully.   b _ _ _

39   You can hear this instrument in many pop songs.   g _ _ _ _ _

40   This may have a blue light and sound like a police car.   a _ _ _ _ _ _ _ _

PART 7

QUESTIONS 41–50

Complete the email.

Write ONE word for each space.

For questions **41–50**, write the words on your answer sheet.

Example: | **0** | was |

| **From:** | Ana |
| **To:** | Tamara |

Yesterday **(0)** ………… my first day back at school. I have missed you **(41)** ………… lot since you moved **(42)** ………… your new school. It's not as much fun in the lessons without you.

(43) ………… you remember Ms Burnford? She's my English teacher this term. She says we **(44)** ………… to read one English book each month **(45)** ………… then write about it. We've got to write in English of course – that's going to **(46)** ………… hard!

Gordana and Sonia are in the class with me again **(47)** ………… year. They asked me to say hello. **(48)** ………… are also many new students in the class this term. I took some photographs **(49)** ………… everyone. I **(50)** ………… going to put them on the internet tomorrow.

Test 3

PART 8

QUESTIONS 51–55

Read the notice and the email.

Fill in the information in Jayden's notes.

For questions **51–55**, write the information on your answer sheet.

Book by 13 March for

SCHOOL TRIP TO
Oasis Water Park

19 March

Bus leaves school 8.30 a.m.
Be here by 8.15 a.m.

Price: £7.50

| From: | Rob |
| To: | Jayden |

You have to book the school trip to the water park before 13th March, so I've done that and I've also paid the £15 for both of us. Don't take any food on the trip, there's a café there, but bring your camera. I'll see you outside the station at 8.00 a.m. – then we can walk to school together.

Jayden's notes

School trip

Trip to: Oasis Water Park

Date: **51**

Cost of trip per person: **52** £

Time bus goes: **53** a.m.

Place to meet Rob: **54**

Take: **55**

PART 9

QUESTION 56

Read the email from your English friend, Alex.

From:	Alex
To:	

Sorry I couldn't come to your birthday meal at the restaurant last night. Who did you go with? What did you have to eat? What presents did you get for your birthday?

Write an email to Alex and answer the questions.

Write **25–35** words.

Write the email on your answer sheet.

PAPER 2 LISTENING (approximately 30 minutes including 8 minutes transfer time)

PART 1

QUESTIONS 1–5

You will hear five short conversations.

You will hear each conversation twice.

There is one question for each conversation.

For each question, choose the right answer (**A**, **B** or **C**).

Example:

Which is the girl's horse?

A   B   C

---

1 What will they do first at the zoo?

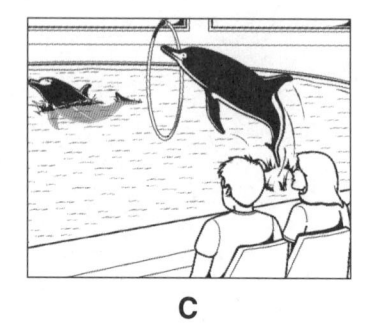

A   B   C

2 Which girl is Crystal?

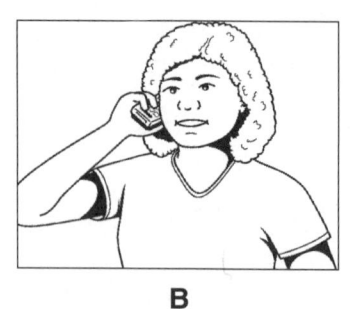

A   B   C

68

Paper 2 Listening

3 What will the boy do at school today?

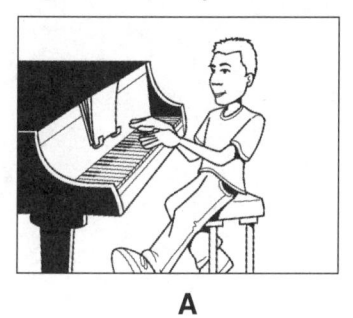

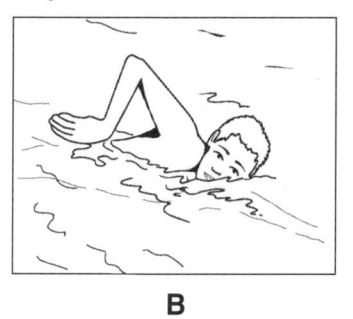

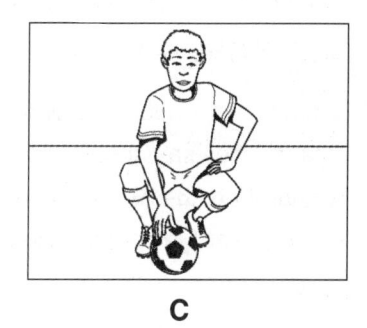

A B C

4 What time did the girl get up?

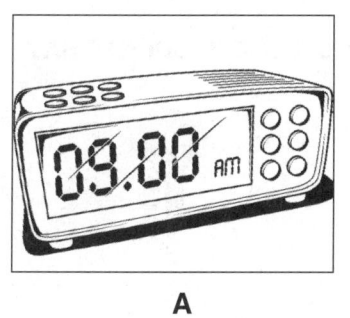

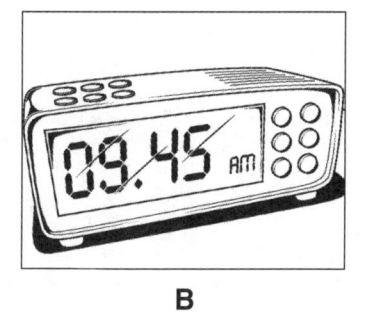

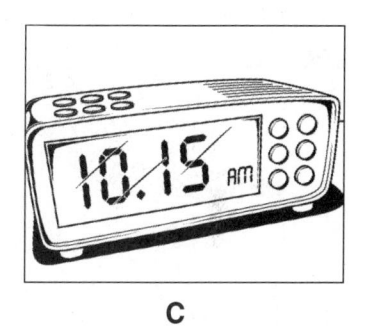

A B C

5 What can Jack eat now?

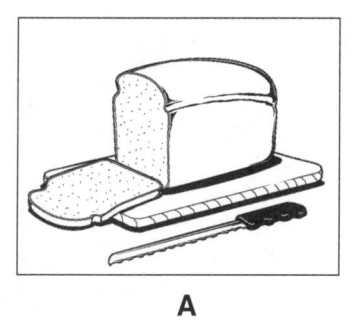

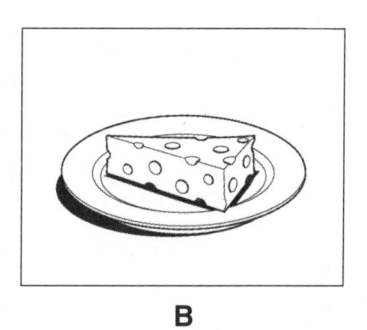

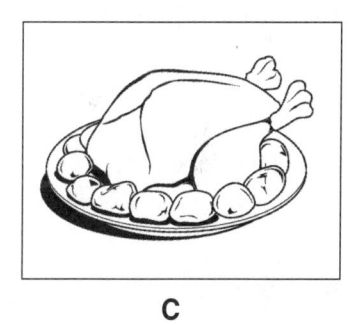

A B C

PART 2

QUESTIONS 6–10

Listen to two students talking about their teachers.
What do they say about each teacher?
For questions **6–10,** write a letter **A–H** next to each person.
You will hear the conversation twice.

Example:

0   Miss Jones   H

PEOPLE		WHAT THE STUDENTS SAY	
6	Mr Benson	A	interesting
7	Mrs Wilson	B	kind
8	Mr Wood	C	old
9	Mrs Barker	D	pretty
10	Mr Davis	E	short
		F	strong
		G	tall
		H	young

PART 3

QUESTIONS 11–15

Listen to a boy, Martin, asking a museum assistant about the museum.

For each question, choose the right answer (**A**, **B** or **C**).

You will hear the conversation twice.

Example:

0   The museum is usually closed on

    A   Sunday.

    B   Monday.

   (**C**) Wednesday.

---

11   You can buy cheap tickets after

    A   3.00 p.m.

    B   5.00 p.m.

    C   7.00 p.m.

12   There is a special group price for

    A   4 people.

    B   6 people.

    C   8 people.

13   The meeting place for the tour is in the

    A   main hall.

    B   museum shop.

    C   exhibition room.

14 The shop sells

    A posters.

    B books.

    C postcards.

15 You can get more information by

    A phoning.

    B looking online.

    C visiting the ticket office.

PART 4

QUESTIONS 16–20

You will hear a boy, Mark, asking his sports teacher about football practice.

Listen and complete each question.

You will hear the conversation twice.

First football practice

Team: A

Date: (16) .... September

Time: (17) .... p.m.

Place: (18) ....

Speak to: (19) Mr ....

Bring: (20) ....

Test 3

PART 5

QUESTIONS 21–25

You will hear a teacher talking about a school trip to an exhibition.
Listen and complete each question.
You will hear the information twice.

School trip – 'Life in Amsterdam' exhibition

Name of museum:	City Museum
You can see:	furniture, (21) .... and clothes
Good for people who enjoy:	(22) art or ....
Date of trip:	(23) .... January
Cost of trip:	(24) £ ....
Give money to:	(25) Mrs ....

You now have 8 minutes to write your answers on the answer sheet.

74

PAPER 3   SPEAKING (8–10 minutes)

The Speaking test lasts 8 to 10 minutes. You will take the test with another candidate. There are two examiners, but only one of them will talk to you. The examiner will ask you questions and ask you to talk to the other candidate.

Part 1 (5–6 minutes)

The examiner will ask you and your partner some questions. These questions will be about your daily life, past experience and future plans. For example, you may have to speak about your school, hobbies or home town.

Part 2 (3–4 minutes)

You and your partner will speak to each other. You will ask and answer questions. The examiner will give you a card with some information on it. The examiner will give your partner a card with some words on it. Your partner will use the words on the card to ask you questions about the information you have. Then you will change roles.

Test 4

PAPER 1   READING AND WRITING (1 hour 10 minutes)

PART 1

QUESTIONS 1–5

Which notice (**A–H**) says this (**1–5**)?
For questions **1–5**, mark the correct letter **A–H** on your answer sheet.

Example:

0   It is cheaper if you visit with a lot of people.   *Answer:*   **0** — B

---

1   You should not wake these animals up.

2   Some visitors must go to the zoo with an older person.

3   You should not get too close to these animals.

4   Do not leave anything behind.

5   The people who work here will give you the information you need.

A   DO NOT GO NEAR THE LIONS' CAGE OR GIVE THEM FOOD

B   **Park Zoo**
Half-price entrance for groups of 20 or more

C   Zoo staff are happy to answer visitors' questions about the animals

D   **Free zoo entrance to children under 8**

E   **City Zoo**
No entrance to under 12s without an adult

F   **Picnic Tables**
Take your empty cans and bags with you

G   Visitors must leave Monkey House one hour before zoo closes

H   **Quiet please!**
Baby hippos need to sleep

PART 2

QUESTIONS 6–10

Read the sentences about a girl's trip to New York.
Choose the best word (**A**, **B** or **C**) for each space.
For questions **6–10**, mark **A**, **B** or **C** on your answer sheet.

Example:

0   Gill was very .... about going to New York.

    A   excited   **B**   special   **C**   fine

Answer: 0 A ■

---

6   Gill was going to .... two weeks with her cousins.

    A   visit   **B**   spend   **C**   pass

7   Gill's cousins came to .... her at the airport.

    A   bring   **B**   catch   **C**   meet

8   On the first day, Gill .... to climb to the top of the Statue of Liberty.

    A   enjoyed   **B**   wanted   **C**   explained

9   They went to lots of famous places so Gill felt .... afterwards.

    A   tired   **B**   heavy   **C**   poor

10   Gill .... for presents for her family in the tourist shops.

    A   watched   **B**   saw   **C**   looked

PART 3

QUESTIONS 11–15

Complete the five conversations.

For questions **11–15**, mark **A**, **B** or **C** on your answer sheet.

Example:

0

Where do you come from?

A New York.
B School.
C Home.

Answer: 0 **A** B C

---

11   Mind you don't break that lamp!

A   I don't mind.
B   Does it work?
C   I'll be careful.

12   Shall we invite Monica to the party, too?

A   If you want.
B   So did I.
C   Here you are.

13   There's a great programme on television tonight.

A   I think it is.
B   I would like one, too.
C   I know, but I'm going out.

14   Could you lend me some money for the swimming pool?

A   It doesn't matter.
B   No problem.
C   Sorry, I haven't.

15   What a great T-shirt you're wearing.

A   Do you like it?
B   What size is it?
C   Can you try it on?

QUESTIONS 16–20

Complete the conversation between two friends.
What does Joe say to Tom?
For questions **16–20**, mark the correct letter **A–H** on your answer sheet.

Example:

Tom: Joe, have you heard of the 'Great Race'?

Joe: 0 .....C.....

Answer: 0 [A][B][■C][D][E][F][G][H]

Tom: Well, it's a running race for under 14s. Would you like to be my partner?

Joe: 16 ....

Tom: It's not until September. We've got plenty of time.

Joe: 17 ....

Tom: Not yet. I want someone to run with me.

Joe: 18 ....

Tom: It's just over 4 km. You can do that, can't you?

Joe: 19 ....

Tom: Great! Are you free tomorrow morning at 8 o'clock?

Joe: 20 ....

Tom: OK. I'll meet you in the park at 9.00.

A I see! Well, is the race very long?

B That's too early! Let's make it a bit later.

C No, I haven't Tom. Why?

D I don't know. I haven't run that far before, but I'd like to try.

E I'm not sure. When is it?

F I've never heard of such a long race.

G That's true. Have you already started practising?

H It starts at half past seven.

PART 4

QUESTIONS 21–27

Read the articles by three teenagers about a book they like.
For questions **21–27**, mark **A**, **B** or **C** on your answer sheet.

A book I like

Jake

I've just read *Nina's School* by James Armitage, who's a writer I didn't know. He's written another book about Nina and because she has such an exciting life, I've decided to read that next. There are long words in the book, but I knew most of them – and I got to the end in just two days! I think young people and adults will read the book because of the cool picture on the front.

Sally

I read *Dark* by Karen Gates, my favourite writer. It's quite a sad story, but I thought it was even better than her last one. The picture on the front tells you the story is about horses, but it's not just about that – it's about people too! There are some hard words in it so I had to use a dictionary – but I've read the story twice now!

Andy

I'm reading *Goodbye* by Philip Tate, which has a great picture on the front. It's a strange story so I wanted to see what happened, but because it's quite long, I haven't finished it yet. I think it's a book for children so I couldn't believe my parents liked it too. My friend thinks the first book by Philip Tate is better. I might read that next but I'm not sure.

Example:

0   Who read the whole book very quickly?

A   Jake
B   Sally
C   Andy

Answer: 0 ■ A □ B □ C

---

21 Who was surprised to find that adults enjoyed the book too?

A   Jake
B   Sally
C   Andy

22 Who read the same book more than once?

A   Jake
B   Sally
C   Andy

23 Who has already chosen a book to read next?

A   Jake
B   Sally
C   Andy

24 Who thought the story in the book was unusual?

A   Jake
B   Sally
C   Andy

25 Who found some of the language in the book difficult to understand?

A   Jake
B   Sally
C   Andy

26 Who believes that the front of the book will make teenagers interested in the story?

A   Jake
B   Sally
C   Andy

27 Who has read other books by the same writer?

A   Jake
B   Sally
C   Andy

PART 5

QUESTIONS 28–35

Read the article about a school trip to a fire station.
Choose the best word (**A**, **B** or **C**) for each space.
For questions **28–35**, mark **A**, **B** or **C** on your answer sheet.

Meeting the fire fighters

My name (**0**) .... Rachel Wild. Last week, my class visited a fire station with our teacher. We met Jim, (**28**) .... works at the fire station. Jim showed us (**29**) .... and told us about his job.

Jim is part of a team of fire fighters called Red Watch. Every morning, he checks (**30**) .... the things in the fire engine to make sure (**31**) .... is missing. Everything must be in (**32**) .... right place. There is also a tall, empty building at the station where Jim (**33**) .... practise climbing in through windows.

Jim let us (**34**) .... in the fire engine and try on the special clothes he wears, (**35**) .... we had to be careful not to start the engine or push the buttons!

Example:

| 0 | A | is | B | are | C | be | Answer: | 0 ■ □ □ |

28	A	what	B	who	C	that
29	A	above	B	among	C	around
30	A	other	B	many	C	all
31	A	nothing	B	anything	C	something
32	A	one	B	the	C	a
33	A	can	B	need	C	should
34	A	sitting	B	sat	C	sit
35	A	or	B	but	C	because

PART 6

QUESTIONS 36–40

Read the descriptions of some words about school.
What is the word for each one?
The first letter is already there. There is one space for each other letter in the word.
For questions **36–40**, write the words on your answer sheet.

Example:

| 0 | You can look in this book if you do not know how to spell a word. | d _ _ _ _ _ _ _ _ _ |

Answer: | 0 | dictionary |

36 You look at this when you are using the computer to see what you have written.   s _ _ _ _ _

37 You go here to have lessons.   c _ _ _ _ _ _ _ _

38 You study this subject to learn about what happened a long time ago.   h _ _ _ _ _ _

39 The teacher writes on this during the lesson.   b _ _ _ _

40 If you study this subject, you will learn about the mountains and rivers of different countries.   g _ _ _ _ _ _ _ _

PART 7

QUESTIONS 41–50

Complete the message put on a teenage website.

Write ONE word for each space.

For questions **41–50**, write the words on your answer sheet.

Example: | **0** | o l d |

My name is Sangita Das and I am thirteen years (**0**) .... I love playing chess. My dad (**41**) .... my older brother, Arjan, also play chess. I started winning against my dad about two years (**42**) .... He does (**43**) .... mind too much!

I practise chess for one (**44**) .... two hours every day – usually on the computer, but sometimes against my brother. He knows (**45**) .... lot about chess. He thinks he's better (**46**) .... me. He may (**47**) .... right. But when he (**48**) .... thirteen he didn't play chess as well (**49**) .... I do now.

One day, I (**50**) .... like to play in an international chess competition – I'm sure I can win!

PART 8

QUESTIONS 51–55

Read the notice and the email.
Fill in the information in Alicia's notes.
For questions **51–55**, write the information on your answer sheet.

Tennis Competition
for 11–14-year-olds

Saturday 14 May
&
Sunday 15 May

5.30 p.m. – 7.30 p.m.

FREE ENTRY

Bandon Tennis Club
Free bus from train station

From:	Jenny
To:	Alicia

I can't go to watch the tennis competition with Maria on Saturday. Do you want to go instead? Her mother will take you both in her car. They will come to your house at 4 o'clock.

It's free so you won't need any money, but don't forget your camera!

Alicia's notes

Tennis competition

Where to go:	Bandon Tennis Club
Who with:	**51**
Date:	**52**
Time begins:	**53** _____ p.m.
What to bring:	**54**
Travel by:	**55**

PART 9

QUESTION 56

Read the email from your English friend, Tony.

From:	Tony
To:	

I'm going to a concert on Friday. What kind of music do you like? Where do you listen to it? What's your favourite band?

Write an email to Tony and answer the questions.

Write **25–35** words.

Write the email on your answer sheet.

PAPER 2 LISTENING (approximately 30 minutes including 8 minutes transfer time)

PART 1

QUESTIONS 1–5

You will hear five short conversations.
You will hear each conversation twice.
There is one question for each conversation.
For each question, choose the right answer (**A**, **B** or **C**).

Example:

Which is the girl's horse?

A B C

1 What will Sophie's father do after work today?

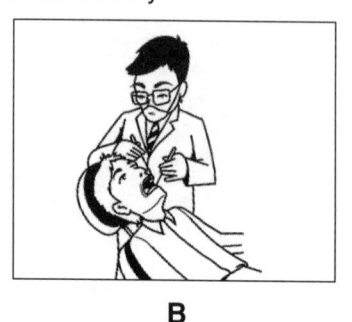

A B C

2 How much did Jake pay for his bicycle?

£85 £90 £150

A B C

3 What is Sam going to wear in the park?

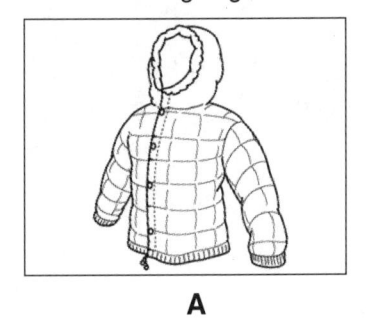

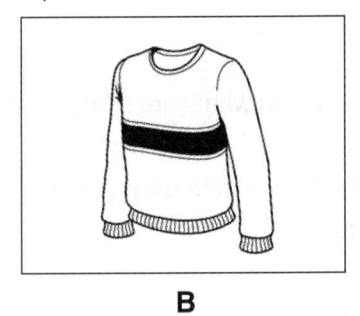

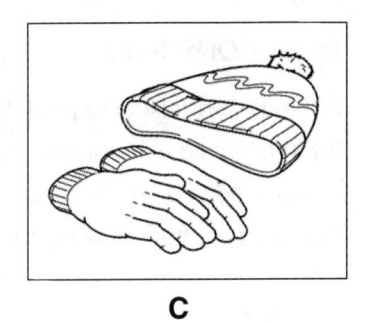

A   B   C

4 What does Amy Gibb look like now?

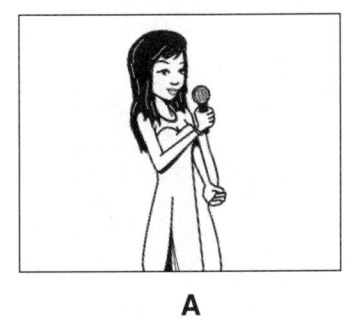

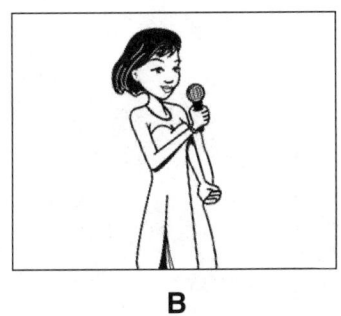

A   B   C

5 At what time will the class start?

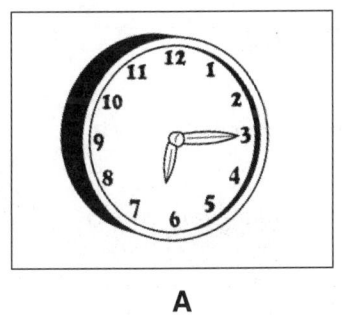

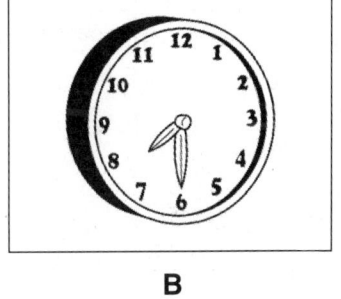

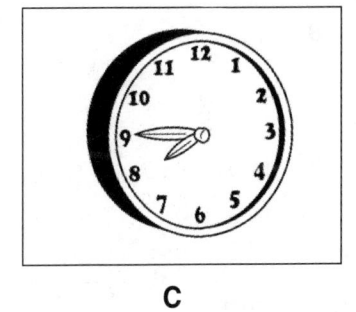

A   B   C

Test 4

PART 2

QUESTIONS 6–10

Listen to Ella talking to her father about what things her friends bought.
What thing did each person buy?
For questions **6–10**, write a letter **A–H** next to each person.
You will hear the conversation twice.

Example:

0   Ella   **A**

PEOPLE		THINGS	
6	Clara	A	bag
		B	book
7	Adam		
		C	cake
		D	CD
8	Yasmin		
		E	chocolates
9	Louis	F	postcards
		G	ring
10	Ryan		
		H	watch

90

PART 3

QUESTIONS 11–15

Listen to Isabel talking to her mother about her new pen-friend.

For each question, choose the right answer (**A, B** or **C**).

You will hear the conversation twice.

Example:

0   Isabel's pen-friend, Miranda, lives in

    A   Germany.

    B   Spain.

    (**C**)   Argentina.

---

11   Miranda's father is

    A   an engineer.

    B   a manager.

    C   a teacher.

12   How many letters has Miranda written to Isabel?

    A   one

    B   two

    C   three

13   Isabel will invite Miranda to visit her in

    A   July.

    B   August.

    C   December.

14 Which is Miranda's favourite sport?

    A baseball

    B basketball

    C tennis

15 Miranda sent Isabel a picture of

    A her brother.

    B her mother.

    C herself.

Paper 2 Listening

PART 4

QUESTIONS 16–20

You will hear a teacher talking to a boy about a school trip to an art exhibition.

Listen and complete each question.

You will hear the conversation twice.

School trip

Name of art exhibition: 'Rainbows'

Day: (16) ....

Leave at: (17) .... p.m.

Cost of trip: (18) £ ....

Bring: (19) ....

Talk by: (20) Alice ....

93

Test 4

PART 5

QUESTIONS 21–25

You will hear a man talking on the radio about a dancing competition.
Listen and complete each question.
You will hear the information twice.

Dancing competition

Dancers must be aged:	12–14 years old
Date:	**(21)** 11th..................................
Place:	**(22)** .... Park School
Starts at:	**(23)** .... p.m.
Colour of clothes:	**(24)** must be..........................
Phone number:	**(25)** ....

You now have 8 minutes to write your answers on the answer sheet.

PAPER 3   SPEAKING (8–10 minutes)

The Speaking test lasts 8 to 10 minutes. You will take the test with another candidate. There are two examiners, but only one of them will talk to you. The examiner will ask you questions and ask you to talk to the other candidate.

Part 1 (5–6 minutes)

The examiner will ask you and your partner some questions. These questions will be about your daily life, past experience and future plans. For example, you may have to speak about your school, hobbies or home town.

Part 2 (3–4 minutes)

You and your partner will speak to each other. You will ask and answer questions. The examiner will give you a card with some information on it. The examiner will give your partner a card with some words on it. Your partner will use the words on the card to ask you questions about the information you have. Then you will change roles.

Visual materials for Paper 3

1A

'Happy Friends'
The newest ice cream shop in town

More than 50 kinds of ice cream –
take away or eat in the shop
10 a.m. – 8 p.m. every day
33 Long Street, Sydney

2B

Music school

- name / school ?
- what / learn ?
- when / classes ?
- classes / £ ?
- address ?

3A

BIKE RACE

Are you 13–16?

Join our race

on Saturday, 6 April

3 p.m.

at the town bridge

Wear a helmet

1st Prize: a new bike!

4B

Film for students

- name / film ?

- Friday ?

- for all classes ?

- start ? 🕐 ?

- where ?

Visual materials

1B

Shop

- name / shop ?
- what / sell ?
- address ?
- new shop ?
- time / close ?

2A

'Stars of Tomorrow'

Music School
26 Baxter Street
We'll teach you to sing and
play an instrument!
Classes every Friday
3 p.m. – 5 p.m.
Fee: £15 a month
Visit: www.music.co.uk

3B

Bike race

- where ?
- date ?
- for teenagers ?
- what / win ?
- what / wear ?

4A

Film for Students
Tuesday 22 April

'Do animals dream?'

For classes 10 and 11

At the Silver Cinema

1.30 p.m. – 2.30 p.m.

Interested? Ask Mr Brown

Visual materials

1C

Candy's Clothes

For teenagers
20 River Street (behind City Bus Station)

Open 10 a.m. – 6 p.m.
(Sundays 10 a.m. – 5 p.m.)
All clothes half price this month
See clothes on our website
at www.candy.com

2D

English speaking practice

- time?
- where?
- for all ages?
- every day?
- who / teacher?

3C

Fun Run

FREE

3 kilometres round the castle
starts at 2 p.m.
Sunday, 20 November

Under 15s only!
Remember to bring water

Phone Mr Jones on 655466

4D

DVDs for sale

- for teenagers ?
- new films ?
- how many ?
- DVDs / £ ?
- more information ?

Visual materials

1D

Clothes shop

- for adults ?

- cheap prices ?

- open / Sundays ?

- where / shop ?

- website address ?

2C

Extra English Speaking Practice
11–14-year-olds

*Every Monday and Wednesday
6-week course
with new English teacher, Mr Green
1–2 p.m.*

Meet in school library

3D

Running race

- when / race ?
- cost ?
- what / bring ?
- how far ?
- more information ? ☎ ?

4C

25 DVDs for sale

Famous films for all the family

£2 each

We have old and new films

Call Ted's Film Shop to
find out more: 662138

Sample answer sheet – Reading and Writing (Sheet 1)

UNIVERSITY of CAMBRIDGE
ESOL Examinations

S A M P L E

Candidate Name
If not already printed, write name in CAPITALS and complete the Candidate No. grid (in pencil).

Candidate Signature

Examination Title

Centre

Supervisor:
If the candidate is ABSENT or has WITHDRAWN shade here

Centre No.

Candidate No.

Examination Details

KET Paper 1 Reading and Writing Candidate Answer Sheet

Instructions

Use a **PENCIL** (B or HB).
Rub out any answer you want to change with an eraser.

For **Parts 1, 2, 3, 4** and **5**:
Mark ONE letter for each question.
For example, if you think **C** is the right answer to the question, mark your answer sheet like this:

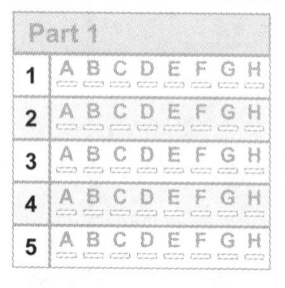

0 A B C

Part 1
1 A B C D E F G H
2 A B C D E F G H
3 A B C D E F G H
4 A B C D E F G H
5 A B C D E F G H

Part 2
6 A B C
7 A B C
8 A B C
9 A B C
10 A B C

Part 3
11 A B C
12 A B C
13 A B C
14 A B C
15 A B C
16 A B C D E F G H
17 A B C D E F G H
18 A B C D E F G H
19 A B C D E F G H
20 A B C D E F G H

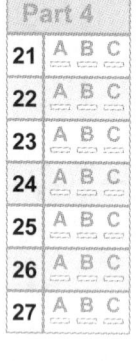

Part 4
21 A B C
22 A B C
23 A B C
24 A B C
25 A B C
26 A B C
27 A B C

Part 5
28 A B C
29 A B C
30 A B C
31 A B C
32 A B C
33 A B C
34 A B C
35 A B C

Turn over for Parts 6 - 9 →

Sample answer sheet – Reading and Writing (Sheet 2)

For **Parts 6, 7 and 8**:
Write your answers in the spaces next to the numbers (36 to 55) like this:

| 0 | example |

Part 6		Do not write here
36		1 36 0
37		1 37 0
38		1 38 0
39		1 39 0
40		1 40 0

Part 7		Do not write here
41		1 41 0
42		1 42 0
43		1 43 0
44		1 44 0
45		1 45 0
46		1 46 0
47		1 47 0
48		1 48 0
49		1 49 0
50		1 50 0

Part 8		Do not write here
51		1 51 0
52		1 52 0
53		1 53 0
54		1 54 0
55		1 55 0

Part 9 (Question 56): Write your answer below.

Do not write below (Examiner use only)

0 1 2 3 4 5

© UCLES 2012 Photocopiable

Sample answer sheet – Listening

UNIVERSITY of CAMBRIDGE
ESOL Examinations

SAMPLE

Candidate Name
If not already printed, write name in CAPITALS and complete the Candidate No. grid (in pencil).

Candidate Signature

Examination Title

Centre

Supervisor:
If the candidate is ABSENT or has WITHDRAWN shade here ▭

Centre No.

Candidate No.

Examination Details

KET Paper 2 Listening Candidate Answer Sheet

Instructions

Use a **PENCIL** (B or HB).

Rub out any answer you want to change with an eraser.
For **Parts 1, 2 and 3**:
Mark ONE letter for each question.
For example, if you think **C** is the right answer to the question, mark your answer sheet like this:

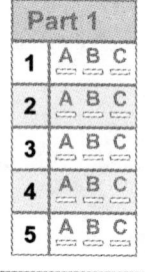

`0 | A B C̶`

Part 1
1 A B C
2 A B C
3 A B C
4 A B C
5 A B C

Part 2
6 A B C D E F G H
7 A B C D E F G H
8 A B C D E F G H
9 A B C D E F G H
10 A B C D E F G H

Part 3
11 A B C
12 A B C
13 A B C
14 A B C
15 A B C

For **Parts 4 and 5**:
Write your answers in the spaces next to the numbers (16 to 25) like this:

`0 | example`

Part 4		Do not write here
16		1 16 0
17		1 17 0
18		1 18 0
19		1 19 0
20		1 20 0

Part 5		Do not write here
21		1 21 0
22		1 22 0
23		1 23 0
24		1 24 0
25		1 25 0

© UCLES 2012 Photocopiable